Creatures
of
Mystery

by
Jan Fortman

A

Book

From

RAINTREE CHILDRENS BOOKS
Milwaukee • Toronto • Melbourne • London

Library of Congress Number: 77-24705

Art and Photo Credits

Cover illustration, Lynn Sweat
Illustrations on pages 7, 14, 33, 36, 39, and 41, James Warhola
Photo on page 10, Tom McHugh, Photo Researchers, Inc.
Photo on page 20, Jerry Hout, National Audubon Society Collection/P.R.
Illustration on page 22, Courtesy of American Museum of Natural History
Photo on page 25, Mitchell Campbell, National Audubon Society Collection/P.R.
Photo on page 30, Lynwood Chace, National Audubon Society Collection/P.R.
Photos on pages 35 and 40, S.H. Gottscho, Courtesy of the American Museum of
    Natural History
Photo on page 38, B.J. Kaston, Courtesy of the American Museum of Natural History
Photo on page 43, Leonard Lee Rue, III, National Audubon Society Collection/P.R.
Photos on pages 45 and 46, Charles J. Ott, National Audubon Society Collection/P.R.
All photo research for this book was provided by Roberta Guerette
Every effort has been made to trace the ownership of all copyrighted material in this
book and to obtain permission for its use.

Library of Congress Cataloging in Publication Data

Fortman, Janis L 1949-
  Creatures of mystery.

  SUMMARY: Describes the curious behavior of salmon, lemmings, whales,
caribou, and insectivorous plants.
  1. Zoology—Miscellanea—Juvenile literature.
2. Animal migration—Juvenile literature. 3. Insectivorous plants—Juvenile
literature. [1. Animals—Miscellanea. 2. Animals—Migration. 3. Insectivorous
plants] I. Title
QL49.F67   596   77-24705
ISBN O-8172-1063-6 lib. bdg.

Manufactured in the United States of America.
ISBN O-8172-1063-6

Contents

Chapter 1

The San Clemente Monster

Everyone has heard of the Abominable Snowman, that huge bear-like "animal" that hides out in the Himalayas. And everyone has heard of the Loch Ness monster, that giant sea creature that lurks in a lake in Scotland. So many stories have been told about these creatures that they have become famous.

But there are many tales about other creatures that are not as well known. These are also creatures of mystery. For example, there is a story of a sea monster off the coast of California.

The story began around 1900. Local fishermen claimed they had seen a huge sea creature near the island of San Clemente, off the California coast. They called it the "San Clemente Monster."

They described the monster as being about twenty feet long and ten feet across. They said it appeared to have black skin and a body shaped like the head of a lizard. The creature didn't have a mouth, but it did have two round, bulging eyes on its head.

The fishermen first saw the monster floating lazily in the water. As they approached it, the monster turned slowly to look at them. Then, suddenly, the creature sank into the sea. It didn't make a splash or cause a ripple in the water as it quickly dropped beneath the surface.

What *was* the "San Clemente Monster"? Was it a whale—a rare kind that scientists know little about? Or was it something else? And what became of it?

No one knows. The "San Clemente Monster" seems to have vanished. Its identity remains a mystery.

Creatures like the "San Clemente Monster," the Abominable Snowman, and the Loch Ness monster are not seen very often. They show themselves just enough to give rise to legends of mysterious beings. We can't explain what they are. But their mysteries fascinate us.

These are not the only creatures of mystery. There are many plants and animals that do strange, often unexplainable things.

There are plants, for example, that at first glance, *appear* to be rather ordinary. But they actually *eat insects*! Why they do this, and *how,* make for an interesting real-life mystery.

There are mysteries concerning the migrations that animals make. For instance, *caribou* (a species of deer) travel each year in groups of thousands across hundreds of miles of Arctic snows. They climb steep mountains and swim fast-flowing rivers in their long and difficult journey. Where are they going? What are they looking for? Why do they make these dangerous trips? Why do they move in such large groups over hundreds of bitter, snowbound miles?

And then there is the mystery of the *lemmings*. Once every four years, tens of thousands of these small mouse-like animals migrate. They rush over fields, swim across lakes, and even pour through towns. They keep moving until they die. Why do they do this? What causes them to make their mad race to nowhere?

And what about the mysterious migration of the *salmon*? These fish swim through thousands of miles of ocean to the land's edge. Then they swim up rivers and streams and climb waterfalls, just to return home! And to die. Why do they make this long and difficult "journey of death"? How do they find their way?

There are still other mysteries in the natural world. Healthy *whales* swim onto beaches and refuse to return to the water. They just lie there, waiting to die. Why do the whales do this? Why do they bring about their own deaths? Let's enter the worlds of these amazing creatures of mystery.

Chapter 2

A Mad Race to Nowhere

It is early spring. The snow is melting in northern Norway—a cold, rough, mountainous land. The waters flow through narrow valleys, down the mountains into the *fjords* (narrow parts of the sea), and finally out to the sea. In the low, damp flats, the melting snow lies in puddles.

Hidden in the long grasses are many round nests of dried grass and mud. These are home to the lemmings—small, mouse-like animals. Only six inches long, lemmings have fat, furry, brown bodies, tiny ears, and small tails. Their legs and arms are very short.

All over the fields, the lemmings sit nervously, chewing blades of grass with their long,

9

yellow teeth. They turn their heads quickly to the right and to the left. Their whiskers twitch. At any strange sound, they scurry to hide in whatever safety they can quickly find.

This year, there are many more lemmings than usual. Their home grassland cannot feed all these hungry little animals. So the lemmings start to spread out. They move in all directions, searching for food. Before they realize it, they have started a strange migration.

For the lemmings, there is no turning back. Once they choose a route and start to travel, they must keep moving in that direction. Noth-

The lemmings make a mad dash for the sea.

ing will stop their movement. Whatever lies in their path, the lemmings will try to cross.

The little animals stop only to eat and then scamper on their way. They tear through fields, destroying everything in sight. Like a huge army, they sweep through the land. One lemming dashes across a field, weaving in and out of the paths of other lemmings. It stops and sniffs, its whiskers moving nervously. It nibbles on a blade of grass, and then it's off again. Quickly it's lost in the army of lemmings marching across the field.

Nothing stops the lemmings! Their race picks up more speed. The little animals tramp through swamps, darting between the long grasses. Quickly they climb up rocky mountains, past short, scraggly pine trees. Half running, half swimming, they tramp through the melting snow waters. Their unstoppable march goes on and on. *Where are they headed?*

The army finally comes to the river. The little animals run up and down the bank, chattering all the while. They are looking for an easy way across. Then one lemming notices a log across the water. He races across it, and the other lemmings follow. In their eagerness to cross, they run into one another. Many lemmings are knocked into the water. Some drown. Others quickly swim to the other side.

The lemmings are perfect targets for their enemies. When the lemming population is this large, all kinds of animals hunt them—even animals that don't generally eat lemmings. Large birds watch from tree branches. Foxes sneak along the banks. Everywhere, their enemies wait.

The lemmings come to a rocky field scattered with caribou. They scamper across the field, running among the legs of the great deer. Many are crushed beneath the caribou's huge, heavy feet.

In spite of all these dangers, the lemmings march on. They pour down the side of a mountain and invade the village below. People scream as the lemmings tear through the streets. Children throw down their bicycles and run into their homes for safety. Thousands of lemmings cover the streets. Many are crushed by cars; many more drown in the streams and rivers that flow through the villages. Then, as suddenly as they appeared, the little animals are gone. All that remain are the dead lemmings that litter the streets and rivers.

The survivors run on and on. They follow the valleys down to the fjords, the narrow fingers of water that poke inland from the sea. And then the whole army halts. Straight ahead lies the sea. Finally, after miles of traveling over mountains, valleys, and streams, the lemmings are now face-to-face with the greatest obstacle of all—the ocean.

Without hesitation the lemmings jump right into the cold waters. To them, the ocean is just another body of water, just another lake or pond. Thousands of the little creatures thrash about, trying to swim their way across the sea.

Some lemmings don't make it very far. Great waves carry them back to shore, flipping them over and over. Finally they're dropped back onto the beach. But thousands of others make it past the waves. Out to sea, the little animals swim through the cold, green water. They cover the surface of the ocean for miles, like a blanket.

A short distance out, a fishing boat bobs in the water. Dozens of lemmings climb up the fishing nets and onto the boat. They rush around the boat in a frenzy—and then they go on. With a great splash, they're back in the water again.

13

The lemmings form a "blanket" on the water. Ships can barely pass through.

The ocean is so thick with lemmings that the fishing boat can hardly move. It takes nearly fifteen minutes for the boat to make its way through the blanket of lemmings. Eventually the boat clears its way and passes on.

The lemmings are good swimmers, but they have already swum some miles. They are losing strength rapidly. Weak and hungry, many of the animals drown. Slowly, they sink into the sea.

Only a few lemmings are left. They no longer form a blanket, but are scattered here and there. They keep swimming on. Some are plucked out of the water by birds.

But soon, these remaining lemmings also become weak. They swim desperately on, with what little strength they have left. But eventually they fail and sink down into the depths of the cold, green water.

The ocean is silent. Where there were thousands of chattering lemmings only a short time before, not one single lemming remains. *Why* have they all gone on this journey of suicide? *What* drove them to destroy themselves?

Normally, lemmings lead a quiet, secret life. They are shy little animals who are afraid of just about everything. They build their nests close to the ground. When they are not searching for food, they hide in their tunnels beneath the ground. They come out only to look for food.

But the lemming population goes through a four-year cycle. During the first two years, the reproduction rate is slow. But in the third year, they have a population explosion! Lemmings then give birth to as many as ten babies at once.

By the fourth year of the cycle, the lemmings are too crowded. There just isn't enough food for all of them. So, an amazing change comes over these shy little animals. Suddenly they become bolder in their search for food.

That's when the migrations start. The little animals leave their nests and invade the land. Over mountains and rivers, through forests and swamps, the lemmings stop at nothing in their search for food. Finally, they reach the sea. There, as we've seen, most of them drown.

What causes these strange actions? *Why* do the lemmings go on these mad migrations? *Why* do they invade the land?

Long ago, people believed that a legendary continent called *Atlantis* might provide an answer to these questions. They believed that this continent once existed off the coast of Europe in the Atlantic Ocean. But, according to the legend, Atlantis suddenly sank into the sea, lost forever. Early scientists thought that perhaps the lemmings jumped into the sea to try to reach Atlantis. But this idea is just part of a legend.

Eskimos had a different answer to these puzzling questions. They believed the lemmings fell down from the heavens during snowstorms. Some Eskimos claimed they even saw this happen. They said they saw the little furry animals drift down among the snowflakes.

Can people do anything to stop this "mad race to nowhere?" Can they keep the lemmings from destroying the land and themselves?

The answer is *no*. Scientists *can* figure out exactly *when* the migration will happen. But they still don't know *how* or *where* it will start. They don't even know where the animals will go. At present, there is nothing that can stop the "suicidal march" of the lemmings.

Chapter 3

The Incredible Journey of Death

The ocean was still. Only a few swells disturbed its calm surface. Below was another world, a world full of life, motion, and color.

Sleek, silver salmon darted back and forth. They flashed through the water as they chased after tiny fish for food. All the time, the fish kept a lookout for whales, sharks, and other dangerous fish. For months, the salmon had been living in this part of the Pacific Ocean. They were not far from the coast of Asia.

The adult salmon were beginning to feel restless. They were overcome with an unexplainable urge to move on. Slowly, they started to move eastward, a little way each day. Gradually, this urge to move east completely took hold of them. They started to swim toward the coast of North America.

At a speed of three or four miles an hour, the salmon swam across thousands of miles of ocean waters. They traveled as much as thirty or forty miles each day. It was an incredible journey!

The salmon were on their way home. The fish were swimming back to their *spawning grounds*—the place of their birth. This seems to be the sole purpose of the Pacific salmon's life—to return home, mate, and then die.

Somehow, from the middle of the great ocean, the salmon were able to choose the right course. The salmon swam across thousands of miles of oceans to the coast of North America. All that time, glands in the salmon's bodies were sending out signals. The signals were telling each fish what it had to do. No matter what the danger, the salmon would not leave its course.

The urge increased as the salmon neared the American coast. *But so did the dangers!* The fish had to dive deep to escape the many birds and sharks. Overhead, eagles circled.

During the long journey home, the salmon's
color changes from silver to bright red.

Thousands of salmon swam together, all heading in the same direction. They were looking for the river they had known as young fish. Somehow the salmon were able to choose the right one. That *right one* was the river they had followed to the ocean in an opposite direction a few years before. That river had taken them from their homes, and now it would take them back.

As the salmon swam past the rivers that flowed into the ocean, they finally chose one river. A male salmon started toward the river's mouth with thousands of others. As he swam into the harbor, he began to taste the fresh water of the stream. He had to keep on guard. Besides all the natural dangers, the salmon now also had to watch for fishing lines and traps.

The male salmon stayed in the harbor for several days, feeding on smaller fish and crabs. He had to build his strength for the journey that was yet to come. Once he left the salt water and entered the river, he would never eat again.

After a few days, the male salmon was ready. Big, strong, and fit, he left the salt water forever to start the hard swim up the river. He entered the fresh river water with thousands of other salmon, all making this same trip home.

The salmon fought against the strong current. Rushing water pushed him back toward the sea. But the salmon pressed onward, against the current, as hard as he could. The fish was fighting not only for his life, but for that incredible moment when he would find his birthplace. He could do nothing *but* fight to reach his home. His whole body told him he must.

After the salmon left the salt water and entered the river, his body began to change. By

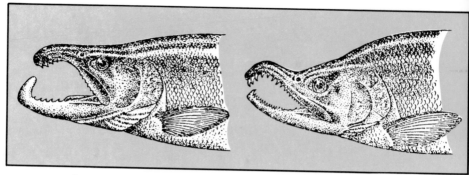

An amazing change comes over the salmon. Is he becoming mean-looking?

the hour, his beautiful silver color was fading. It was being replaced by a bright red. His back was developing humps, and his teeth grew larger. Amazingly, the fish became mean-looking.

When the salmon reached a still pool near the river bank, he rested there. He knew what lay in the distance. Ahead was a high waterfall, and he would need all his strength to climb it.

Just then, a nearby sound startled the fish. A large brown bear dipped its head into the pool and grabbed a salmon with its teeth. Then the bear scampered away to eat its prize.

Minks sneaked along the banks, catching fish almost as large as themselves. Overhead, ravens spent their days fishing and squawking. The birds' wings flapped wildly as they grabbed salmon from the water.

The male salmon managed to keep safe from these enemies. Having rested, he was now ready to attempt the waterfall. He fought the current, made his way around the rocks, and finally reached the bottom of the falls. The water was thundering down, foaming and shooting spray into the air.

The salmon began its leap up the falls. It was like climbing steep stairs. The fish slowly climbed from pool to pool. All the time, water rushed at him, pushing him back down. He had climbed almost to the top, when he was finally driven back down to the bottom again. The salmon slid back into the lowest pool, away from the powerful, falling water. There he rested, gathering up his strength for another try.

After a few minutes, he tried again. He headed back into the waterfall. With all his might, the salmon leaped from the water, arching his back into the shape of a bow. Thrusting with his tail, he shot through the air. Quickly, the fish straightened its body and, with lightning speed, flew over the top of the falls. There he landed in the water that was rushing down to the falls, and he had to swim hard into the current. At last he reached the safety of a quiet pool where he could rest for a while. But, this journey was far from over.

Many of the other salmon were not able to climb the falls. Some kept getting pushed back, again and again, becoming weaker each time. Determined, they kept trying. Some succeeded. But many died in the attempt.

For days the male salmon kept swimming. He forced his way against the fast-moving water, over falls, and through the many rapids. Every so often, he rested in a pool. Then he would push on. The urge for home got even stronger as he drove himself closer and closer.

At the same time, the male salmon was steadily losing his strength. He was using up his store of fat quickly, and he was getting thinner. But with each ounce of strength, he moved closer to his destination.

Finally, one day, the salmon's senses sharpened. He recognized the smell and taste of a little pool. He had reached his spawning grounds! The long journey was finally at an end. Strangely, the salmon now became angry and mean. He chased away other male salmon. He was looking for a mate.

The journey up the waterfall weakens the salmon.

Not far ahead was a female salmon, green in color. She was busy digging out a nest with her tail. The male salmon swam over and waited nearby. He angrily bit the tail of any other male that dared come near.

It took the female salmon several days to build the nest. All that time, the male salmon patiently stood guard. Finally, the female signaled that she was ready. She sank into the nest, and was joined by her mate. The mating took place very quickly. Then the female salmon covered her nest and swam away. She had to start another nest and mate with another male salmon. Female salmon make four separate nests. When the fourth nest has been completed, the female salmon dies.

Soon, the eggs she left will hatch, and many more young salmon will make their way for thousands of miles to the sea. In time, they will repeat the journey home that their parents made.

The male salmon swam away. He was now old and tired, and he swam slowly away from the nest where he had mated. There was nothing left for him to do. He had no interest in anything. As he drifted with the current, he no longer tried to swim against it. There was no reason to—his journey had been completed.

The current caught hold of him and pulled him down to the falls. It pushed the dying fish over, dropping him on a rock. The salmon flapped his tail with the little life he had left. And then he stopped fighting. He had made the journey he was born to make, and now his life was over.

From deep in the Pacific, almost as far away as Asia, the salmon had returned home. What an incredible journey it had been! No other species of fish could make such a journey. No other fish could swim thirty miles a day through the ocean. No other fish could fight the current, one hundred miles upstream.

Not even all the salmon could finish this incredible journey. Only one-tenth of one percent ever made it home. Only the strongest and fittest fish completed the trip. The others died along the way. They died either because they were too weak or because they were caught by other animals from the land, the sky, and the water.

What is the mysterious force that pulls the salmon home at all costs and in the face of unbelievable dangers?

It remains a mystery because no one can explain it. It must be *instinct*—an unthinking knowledge that salmon are born with. Some kind of chemical signal inside the salmon's bodies must tell them what to do.

How do the fish find their way? Scientists only know part of the answer. They know that salmon are able to *smell* their way through fresh-water streams. Each stream has a different smell. Humans can't smell these differences, but salmon can. Their sense of smell is very highly developed.

But what about the salmon's incredible journey through the ocean? How do they find their way to the mouth of a river thousands of miles away? Do they again use their keen sense of smell?

Some scientists think so. But others believe that salmon's sense of smell just isn't *that* strong. Besides, say many scientists, salmon can't smell in salt water. Not until the fish reach fresh water does their sense of smell take over.

Some scientists believe that salmon use the sun or moon to find their way through the ocean waters. They believe the fish somehow remember the exact angles of the sun or moon when they made the opposite journey years before. But are fish able to store memories?

Remember, these are only guesses. How salmon find their way through the ocean, and what forces drive them on this incredible journey, still remain a mystery.

Chapter **4**

The Burial Ground of the Whales

The sun shone brightly on the white sand. Palm trees swayed in the breeze. Along the beach, people bathed in the Florida sun. The blue-green ocean was still, and the waves rolled gently into shore.

Suddenly huge black shapes appeared in the water. They were moving quickly, heading for shore.

Everyone stopped what they were doing. People ran to the water and watched with surprise. Whales hardly ever swam this close to shore. Never had the people seen so many whales at one time!

Closer and closer the whales swam. They were a herd of *pilot whales*. There were dozens of them—dozens of sleek, black bodies swimming toward shore. The whales glided swiftly into the shallow water off the beaches.

Then one whale slid out of the water and onto the sand. There it lay, half in the water and half out. Its black body glistened in the sun. The whale lay very still, like a huge rock on the sand.

Then another whale slid out of the water, and then another. One by one, the whales slid onto the beach.

The whales beached themselves to prepare for death.

But what were the whales doing? Whales can't survive for long out of water. They need water in order to live. Even though they have lungs, they also breathe through the many pores in their skin. Without water, the pores dry up and the whales can't breathe.

Knowing this, the people rushed over to the whales. They ran into the shallow water to try to save the whales. They pushed and tugged at the huge animals, trying to move them back into the water. But each whale weighed thousands of pounds! It took many people to move just one whale even a foot or two.

Still, the people pushed and tugged. But the large animals fought against them. They flapped their tails wildly, often hitting people and knocking them down. For some strange reason, the whales *didn't want* to return to the water.

Finally, a group of people managed to push one whale out into the water. But the whale didn't swim out to sea. Instead, it slid back again onto the beach.

Then a Florida Marine Patrol boat arrived. People helped the Patrol crew tie ropes around a whale's tail. The whale struggled to get free, flapping its tail wildly. Finally, the ropes were tightly fastened. The Patrol boat pulled the huge animal into the water.

But as soon as the animal was set free, it swam right back to shore. There, once again, it slid out of the water. It lay on the sand, peacefully waiting for death.

The people tied whale after whale to the boat and pulled them out to sea. One by one, they released the animals in deep water. A few of the whales swam away. But many just returned to shore.

Why did the whales want to die? *Why* did they swim onto the sand? And *why* did they swim back to the beach after being set free? Was it instinct? Were the animals sick?

We don't know the answers. But this scene in Florida was not unusual. Some scientists believe the whales might have chased schools of fish too close to shore and gotten stranded on the beaches. But if that were true, why would the animals rush right back to shore?

Other scientists believe the whales were in a state of panic. Perhaps sharks or dangerous

killer whales were nearby. Afraid of being at-
tacked by these large sea animals, the whales
swam away quickly. In their fright, they swam to
the shore.

There is a third possibility. Perhaps it was
an instinct like the lemmings' that drove the
whales to shore to die.

Creatures of mystery aren't only found in
the animal kingdom. There are many mysteries
found among the plants in forests and marshes.
The *sundew* and *Venus fly trap* are two plants of
mystery. Our next chapter will explain why.

No matter what was tried, the whales refused to go back into the
water.

The Killer Plants

The sun is low over a swamp in North Carolina. Long grasses and cattails stand in the muddy bottom. The brownish water is still, but the swamp is alive with the sound of spring.

Many plants of all sizes stand in the muddy brown water. A group of tall plants have bright red-purple leaves. They are called *pitcher plants* because the long leaves are shaped like pitchers.

A robin flies over the pitcher plants. She is busy picking insects from the air. Suddenly she notices a fly trapped inside the pitcher of one of the plants. The robin dives down. With her sharp beak, she rips the plant open. She reaches down and plucks out the fly.

A fly buzzes through the muggy air. He lands on a cattail and cleans his face with his tiny arms. Then he flies off again, in search of food.

As the fly passes over the tall pitcher plants, he smells something very sweet, like the nectar

Although beautiful, the pitcher plant is deadly!

of a flower. Interested, the fly sweeps down to investigate.

The fly lands quickly on the lip of the pitcher plant and finds it as soft as velvet. The leaves smell as sweet as honey. The fly follows the scent, walking on the soft mat. The sweet smell becomes stronger and stronger as the fly walks onto the pitcher-shaped leaf. The fly suddenly becomes light-headed.

The fly walks further into the pitcher, but he staggers a little and starts to lose his footing. The fly falls down a long, dangerous tube into darkness inside the plant. His legs touch the smooth, slippery sides of the tube, but he only slides faster. He tries to gain control of his wings, but he's moving too rapidly.

Splash! The fly lands at the bottom of the pitcher, into foul-smelling water. What happened to the sweet smell that had attracted him to the plant?

His wings now wet, the insect can't fly out. The light-headed fly staggers and slips as he tries

The flies don't know what horrible fate awaits them.

to reach the side of the pitcher. Finally, he makes it. He tries to climb up the side, but it's too slippery. Again he slides down and lands in the water with a splash. The fly is trapped.

As time goes by, the fly becomes weaker and weaker. The water inside the plant contains a drug-like substance that slowly overcomes him. Finally, the little insect drowns and floats on the water. Slowly, the watery digestive juices of the plant start to work on the fly's body, taking its nutrients into the plant. This process takes a few days.

Meanwhile, the swamp world goes on. Water spiders skim the surface of the shallow water. Nearby is a tiny plant, just one inch wide. The red tips of its small, paddle-shaped leaves glitter like diamonds in the sun. The plant is called *sundew* because its tips look like dew drops.

A mosquito buzzes through the air. The insect swoops down, looking for food. She notices the glistening sundew leaf. The curious insect lands on the leaf. She starts to walk, but finds the surface of the leaf sticky. The insect can't seem to move her legs.

The mosquito struggles to pull her leg free, but she only gets the other one stuck. The insect's movements trigger the leaf into action.

Above her head, the mosquito sees hundreds of tiny hairs start to bend over her. The insect continues to struggle, desperately trying to get out. But now she's completely stuck. Her wings are also caught on the sticky surface! The insect is trapped. There is no escape. That inviting little leaf was really coated with glue!

The hundreds of tiny hairs bend over the trapped insect, touching her with their deadly tips. Slowly the hairs start to drain the juices from the insect's body. Within ten minutes, the mosquito is dead.

The sundew makes good use of its deadly hairs.

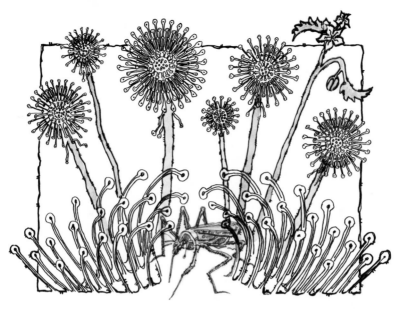

Once the hairs trap the mosquito, it will suddenly disappear.

The hairs of the sundew continue to drain the dead insect. Digestive juices break down the insect's tissues, and slowly the insect is digested.

After several days, the hairs will bend slowly outward. There will be absolutely no trace of the mosquito. The sundew will be ready for its next victim.

Nearby is yet another killer plant, waiting for a victim. Called the *Venus fly trap*, this small plant lies close to the ground. It's only six inches wide.

The plant is a cluster of small stems. At the tip of each stem are two spoon-shaped leaves that are hinged together. These spoons are re-

39

The Venus fly trap waits to close its spines on unsuspecting flies.

ally a trap. The edges of the spoons are lined with sharp spines. In the center of each spoon are three hairs that act as triggers. They tell the plant when there's something in the trap. But an insect must touch two different hairs, or one hair twice, before the trap will shut.

The trap lies open, waiting for something to eat. The inside of the trap is colored bright red.

A few ants climb up the stem of the plant, looking for food. One ant moves onto the red, spoon-shaped leaf. She walks around the edge of the leaf, then slowly makes her way toward the center. Little does the ant know how close she is to death.

The ant continues to walk slowly around the leaf, looking for food. Suddenly she brushes past one of the hairs! All she needs to do now is touch one again—and the trap will close! Only if she doesn't touch a trigger hair will the ant be safe!

But then the ant brushes against a second hair.

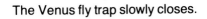
The Venus fly trap slowly closes.

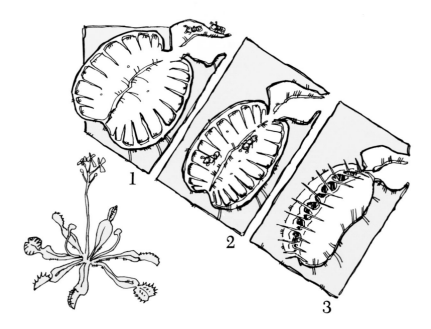

There! That's the signal to the plant that an insect is on the leaf. Quickly the trap snaps shut, crushing the insect. Death is quick.

The same glands that colored the leaf red now start to pour out digestive juices. Slowly they begin to digest the ant.

Why do these plants eat insects? Animals are supposed to eat plants, aren't they? And plants are supposed to get their nutrients from the soil. That's the way it usually is. So why do these plants in a North Carolina swamp eat insects? Scientists are not sure, but they think it has to do with the soil.

Generally, plants get food and water from the soil. But the soil in this North Carolina swamp, as in most swamps, is very poor. It doesn't have the nutrients plants need to grow. The insects provide the plants with the nutrients that are missing in the soil.

But how do these "killer plants" do their deadly work? How is the Venus fly trap able to snap shut? What makes the sundew's hundreds of hairs bend down to trap an insect? Scientists still don't know the answers. These plants don't have muscles or nerves, as animals do. There must be some other way these traps and hairs are triggered—a way we don't understand.

Chapter 6

A Voyage
of Mystery

The Arctic world is colored white. The bare landscape is covered with deep white snow.

Nothing seems to move. But suddenly a form appears on the north horizon. Slowly it moves over the bare land, growing larger and larger all the time. It looks like a reindeer, with large, heavy antlers. This animal is a caribou.

As the great animal makes its way across the snow, another shape appears behind it. The second caribou follows the tracks of the first. Then another caribou appears, and another.

Soon there are hundreds of caribou —hundreds of large brown reindeer with huge antlers. And still they keep coming, covering this once empty land.

As quickly as they appear, they are gone. The caribou disappear over the far horizon, headed south. The once pure white land is now gray and scarred with tracks. The animals have left their mark on the land. They move on, driven by some mysterious force.

Where are the caribou going? They are headed for their *calving grounds.* All the caribou in the whole area join together in this great journey south. They will travel hundreds of miles together to reach their calving grounds. There the cows will give birth to their young. After a few short weeks, all the caribou—even the young calves—will begin the long journey back to the Arctic—back to their winter home.

It had been a cold, bitter winter in northern Canada. The icy winds had blasted the temperature down as low as sixty degrees below zero. But with their extra-thick fur, the caribou were able to stand the cold.

The caribou must return to their mating ground.

A female caribou stood alone in the bare white land. She pawed the snow, searching for reindeer moss. Hour after hour, she pawed the deep snow. She moved slowly, ever searching for food.

A wolf howled. Immediately the caribou stopped pawing. She lifted her great head and stood very still. She listened to the wolf. Then she started eating again. The wolf was no danger to her, for she was a strong, healthy animal.

As the days grew longer, this restlessness became stronger. She kept moving south, covering longer distances each day. Soon trees appeared in small patches, black dots on the white snow. She saw other caribou and joined them.

Each day, more and more animals joined the group. The restlessness grew, and the herd began to move faster.

Week after week, the animals continued their journey south. They swam across fast-flowing rivers. If they couldn't cross directly, they swam up or downstream, crossing where they could. On and on they moved, covering as many as thirty miles a day.

The caribou eventually neared a steep mountain. They climbed the sheer, rocky cliff. They moved through the narrow pass. Moving in single file, the animals wore a path over the mountain. Their grunting sounds and clicking hooves could be heard for miles.

As the animals started to near the calving grounds, the female caribou became excited. She speeded up and passed some male caribou. Rushing ahead, all the females arrived at the calving grounds first.

There were already large groups of caribou cows moving around, searching for food. The female left the group. She walked to an empty

This young calf will now join the great trek.

spot and lay down. A few minutes later, she stood up again. On the ground lay the red-brown shape of her newly born calf.

Within a week, most of the calves were born. Then the males arrived. All the caribou for hundreds of miles were gathered in this spot.

At the end of the summer, the caribou began to move north. Once again the great herd flowed over the land. Once again they swam through rivers.

They began their trek north in almost constant sun. No sooner did the sun sink beneath the horizon than it popped up again. The caribou had no relief from the hot sun—and the mosquitos and flies that it brought.

As time passed and the great herd moved further north, the blizzards began. Still the animals trudged on. Slowly the large herd began to break up, each caribou going its own way. Where they had joined in the spring, now they separated.

The female forced her way through the falling snow, her calf beside her. She stopped only to paw beneath the snow for reindeer moss. She was nearing her winter home.

Why do the caribou do this? *Why* do they travel hundreds of miles just to bear their young—only to begin to trace their steps back again a few weeks later?

Very little is known about this voyage of mystery. No one really knows where each herd goes. But many scientists believe each herd always returns to the same spot each year to bear its young.

But *why* do the animals go there? Some scientists believe the animals go there to get away from wolves and insects that would attack the calves.

Perhaps the animals had to go that far to find food. These animals eat mostly reindeer moss. But this moss grows very slowly. It takes twenty to forty years to grow! If the caribou ate all the reindeer moss in a certain spot, they would have to go somewhere else to find food. It's possible that in certain years the animals were forced to find food as far south as Maine.

But these are only guesses. No one really knows. And it seems the caribou will always take their voyage of mystery.